Tong

Travel Guide 2024

A Comprehensive Travel Guide to Exploring Landscapes, Scenic Beauty, Rich Heritage, Hidden Gems, and Cultural Wonders, Alongside Insider Tips for a Memorable Vacation in the South Pacific

Stanley P. Thayer

Table of Contents

INTRODUCTION

Welcome to Tonga

Tonga, a stunning archipelago nestled in the South Pacific, delivers a warm and colorful welcome to everyone who desires to experience its natural beauty. Comprising 169 islands, Tonga is a tropical paradise that captivates tourists with its pristine nature, rich cultural past, and friendly population. As you step onto the beaches of this Pacific beauty, expect to be engulfed by a unique blend of traditional Polynesian charm and contemporary island life.

Overview of Tonga

Situated southeast of Fiji, Tonga remains the last Polynesian nation, keeping its regal history and traditions. The archipelago is structured into four primary island groups: Tongatapu, 'Eua, Ha'apai, and Vava'u. Each group boasts its distinct character, from the bustling capital city of Nuku'alofa in Tongatapu to the pristine natural beauty of the Ha'apai islands. With a tropical climate, crystal-clear waters, and lush landscapes, Tonga boasts a broad range of activities, making it a wonderful spot for both adventure seekers and those seeking a tranquil vacation.

Cultural Etiquette and Customs

Understanding and respecting Tonga's cultural etiquette is vital for an interesting vacation experience. The residents, famous for their kindness, place major significance on old ceremonies. Visitors should be careful of traditional greetings, such as the usual pushing of noses known as the "ha." Modesty in clothes is recommended, especially in more rural regions.

Participating in a kava ceremony, a traditional social gathering, is a unique opportunity to connect with people and discover the cultural value of this ceremonial drink. By respecting these conventions, travelers not only show respect but also open doors to real interactions that represent the heart and spirit of Tonga.

Travel Tips and Safety Information

Navigating Tonga with ease involves a few essential travel recommendations and a thorough grasp of safety issues. Begin by understanding the local money, the Tongan Pa'anga, and be prepared for a cash-centric economy, especially in more remote regions. Health precautions, including vaccination recommendations, are crucial, and travelers are recommended to carry a basic medical kit.

While crime rates are quite low, it's essential to exercise care and safeguard personal goods. Additionally, keeping informed on weather conditions, particularly during cyclone season, ensures a safe and happy journey. Whether you're exploring crowded markets, going on a snorkeling adventure, or immersing yourself in Tonga's traditional festivities, these travel recommendations will enrich your experience and contribute to a memorable stay in this South Pacific sanctuary.

Tonga welcomes travelers with open arms, urging them to explore the beauties of its islands, experience its rich cultural past, and soak in the warmth of its people. As we move deeper into this travel guide, each segment will disclose the layers of Tonga's beauty, offering a way for an exciting adventure throughout the heart of the Pacific.

PLANNING YOUR TRIP

Best Time to Visit

Choosing the perfect time to visit Tonga is crucial for witnessing its distinctive characteristics. The finest time to visit this South Pacific beauty is during the dry season, which generally stretches from May to October. During these months, the weather is temperate, and the islands are showered in sunshine, creating great settings for outdoor activities like snorkeling, diving, and hiking. Be mindful of the cyclone season from November to April, when tropical storms may hinder travel plans. Each season gives a special charm, so tailoring your holiday to fit your preferences and selected activities will ensure a successful and happy journey.

Visa Requirements

Before traveling on your Tongan trip, acquaint yourself with the visa requirements. Most people may enter Tonga for up to 31 days without a visa, but it's crucial to check the newest legislation and verify your eligibility. Extensions may be authorized for a longer stay, and it's vital to check admission requirements with the Tongan immigration officers or the nearest Tongan embassy or consulate before your visit. Ensure your passport is valid for at least six months beyond your projected departure date to avoid any complications during your stay.

Currency and Money Matter

Tonga's currency is the Tongan Pa'anga (TOP), and understanding the local money and banking system is crucial for a smooth vacation. While major credit cards are accepted in urban areas, it's vital to carry some cash, especially when traveling into more remote locales where cash transactions are prevalent. ATMs are accessible in large towns, allowing a simple way to withdraw local currency. Familiarize yourself with current currency rates to make intelligent financial decisions, and consider alerting your bank of your trip dates to prevent any issues with card purchases.

Health and Vaccination Information

Ensuring your health and well-being during your Tonga vacation starts with diligent preparation. Check the Centers for Disease Control and Prevention (CDC) and World Health Organization (WHO) recommendations for vaccines and health measures. Common vaccinations include Hepatitis A and B, typhoid, and routine immunizations.

Travelers should also be wary of the probable threat of mosquito-borne diseases such as dengue fever, therefore packing bug repellent and wearing long sleeves and pants in the evenings is advisable. Consult with your healthcare expert well in advance of your vacation to discuss any additional health problems and obtain particular suggestions depending on your medical history.

Language and Communication

The official languages of Tonga are Tongan and English, and while many people speak English, acquiring a few basic Tongan phrases may improve your cultural experience and make pleasant relationships. "Malo e lelei" (hello) and "ofa atu" (goodbye) are usual greetings, and expressing appreciation with a "fa'afetai" would be greatly appreciated. Embracing the local language indicates a real interest in the culture, making your encounter more interesting and fulfilling.

Packing Tips

Packing for Tonga demands a balance of tropical fundamentals and practical stuff for varied activities. Lightweight, breathable clothing is essential, coupled with a swimsuit, a hat, and sunscreen for sun protection. If you plan on exploring Tonga's undersea wonders, take snorkeling gear, including a mask and fins. Hiking fanatics should carry sturdy footwear for enjoying the beautiful scenery.

Additionally, a travel adapter for electrical outlets, a reusable water bottle, and a basic medical kit could be beneficial during your stay. Check the weather forecast for your particular vacation dates to alter your packing list properly and ensure you are well-prepared for the delights that await in Tonga.

In conclusion, meticulous planning is the cornerstone of a successful Tongan expedition. By picking the ideal time to go, knowing visa requirements, addressing currency challenges, prioritizing health precautions, embracing language differences, and packing smartly, you set the stage for a seamless and pleasant exploration of Tonga's charms.

GETTING THERE

International Airports

Tonga is accessible via its principal international gateway, Fua'amotu International Airport (TBU), located on the main island of Tongatapu. This modern airport accommodates international flights, drawing people from throughout the globe. Fua'amotu International Airport offers vital services, such as currency exchange, automobile rentals, and duty-free outlets, ensuring a smooth transition for arriving and departing passengers. The airport's strategic location in Tongatapu makes it a suitable starting point for seeing the many island groups that constitute the Kingdom of Tonga.

Airlines Serving Tonga

Several reputable airlines connect Tonga to major global hubs, presenting a range of possibilities for travelers. Flag airline Air Tonga serves local flights, while international carriers like Fiji Airways, Virgin Australia, and Air New Zealand offer direct services to Fua'amotu Foreign Airport. These airlines run regular flights, making it very uncomplicated for passengers to schedule their excursions to Tonga. Checking for seasonal offers and flexible travel dates can aid in obtaining cost-effective tickets, guaranteeing that your arrival in Tonga is both straightforward and affordable.

Entry and Exit Procedures

Navigating entry and exit customs is a crucial component of a stress-free travel vacation to Tonga. Most passengers may acquire a visa on arrival for up to 31 days, but it's vital to verify the newest immigration requirements before traveling. Prepare the required papers, including a valid passport, proof of further travel, and any applicable visas.

Customs restrictions forbid the entry of specific products, therefore acquaint yourself with these limitations to avoid any complications upon arrival. Departure formalities are typically easy, with a departure tax required at the airport. Ensuring compliance with entry and exit rules enables a flawless passage in and out of the Kingdom.

Transportation Within Tonga

Once you've arrived in Tonga, navigating between islands and exploring local destinations involves an understanding of the numerous transportation possibilities. Inter-island flights, operated by firms like Real Tonga Airlines, connect the major island groups, enabling a simple means of travel. Additionally, ferry services operate between Tongatapu, Ha'apai, and Vava'u, giving an extra method of transportation with excellent marine views.

In major regions, taxis and rental autos are available, offering flexibility for exploring at your own pace. For a more immersive experience, consider leasing a scooter or bicycle to tour the smaller islands. Engaging with local transportation strengthens your connection with the culture, allowing you to observe Tonga from the viewpoint of its people.

In conclusion, travel to Tonga is facilitated by its international airports, offered by renowned airlines that connect the Kingdom to significant worldwide centers. Navigating admission and exit formalities with thorough preparation offers a hassle-free arrival and departure experience.

Once on Tongan territory, several transportation alternatives await, enabling the chance to explore the varied landscapes and bustling communities that make up this South Pacific treasure. Whether you choose to fly over the islands or sail over the turquoise waters, the travel within Tonga is as intriguing as the destination itself.

ACCOMMODATION

Types of Accommodations

Tonga offers a diverse range of customers, giving several hotels to meet all interests and budgets. From beautiful resorts to simple guesthouses, travelers may select the type of hotel that suits their vacation style. The basic categories of accommodations in Tonga include:

Resorts and Hotels: Tonga boasts a selection of quality resorts and hotels, particularly in popular tourist areas like Nuku'alofa, Vava'u, and Ha'apai. These enterprises usually combine beachfront settings, luxurious facilities, and world-class services, delivering a lavish vacation for customers desiring a pampered experience.

Guesthouses and Bed & Breakfasts: For a more intimate and local experience, guesthouses and bed & breakfasts are strewn around the islands. Run by friendly people, these hotels give personalized attention, welcoming atmospheres, and a chance to immerse yourself in Tongan culture.

Budget Accommodations: Backpackers and budget-conscious vacationers will find several affordable choices, including hostels and budget motels. While these rooms may be lower in amenities, they present a cost-effective solution for persons stressing savings without losing comfort.

Holiday Homes and Villas: Tonga offers vacation homes and villas for those wishing more seclusion and independence. These accommodations are often built with kitchen capabilities, making them suitable for families or groups looking to create a home-away-from-home feel.

Top Hotels and Resorts

Tonga's top hotels and resorts stand as beacons of luxury, delivering tourists with unsurpassed comfort and service. In Nuku'alofa, the capital city, the likes of the Tanoa International Dateline Hotel give a blend of luxury and Pacific beauty.

For an exceptional holiday, resorts such as Fafa Island Resort in the Ha'apai group include overwater bungalows and lovely beaches, creating an amazing environment for relaxation. The Vava'u archipelago is home to resorts like Mystic Sands, where spectacular scenery and world-class amenities define the guest experience. These top-tier hotels ensure that travelers may wallow in grandeur while surrounded by Tonga's natural beauty.

Budget-Friendly Options

Tonga caters to budget-conscious travelers, giving a range of affordable hotels without compromising on quality. Hostels like the Backpackers Townhouse in Nuku'alofa have communal bedrooms and public spaces, creating a busy setting for mingling. Budget hotels, such as the Little Italy Hotel in Vava'u, give clean and comfortable rooms at low costs. Additionally, various guesthouses dispersed among the islands provide affordable alternatives with a local touch, allowing travelers to stretch their budgets while enjoying the warmth of Tongan hospitality.

Unique Stays and Cultural Experiences

For those desiring a more immersive and culturally rich experience, Tonga offers unique accommodations that go beyond regular hotels. Cultural homestays allow living with local families, joining in daily activities, and receiving insights into Tongan culture. Eco-resorts, like Matafonua Lodge in Ha'apai, offer sustainable and nature-focused lodgings, allowing tourists to engage with the environment and contribute to conservation efforts. Staying in a fale, a traditional Tongan house affords a unique glimpse into the local culture and develops a greater appreciation for the Kingdom's rich cultural past.

In conclusion, Tonga's hotel selections cater to the diverse expectations of tourists, ranging from opulent resorts to budget-friendly guesthouses and culturally enriching experiences. Whether you prefer the pleasure of a luxury resort or the authenticity of a homestay, Tonga promises that your choice of accommodation improves your overall travel experience in this Pacific paradise.

DESTINATIONS IN TONGA

Nuku'alofa (Capital City)

1. Attractions

Nuku'alofa, the bustling capital of Tonga, fascinates travelers with a blend of rich traditional heritage and modern influences. The Royal Palace, an architectural marvel, stands as a symbol of the Kingdom's history and serves as the official residence of the queen.

The Royal Tombs, a short distance away, give a calm location and insights into Tonga's royal ancestry. The vibrant Talamahu Market provides a sensory feast with its bright stalls providing local veggies, crafts, and traditional Tongan attire. St. Mary's Cathedral, with its beautiful construction, displays the significant importance of Christianity in Tongan culture. Exploring these places in Nuku'alofa provides a deep glimpse into the heart of the Kingdom.

2. Dining and Nightlife

Nuku'alofa boasts a broad culinary scene, with several dining choices that appeal to all palates. Seafood connoisseurs may enjoy fresh catches at seaside eateries, while guests seeking local flavors may appreciate traditional Tongan cuisine at family-run cafés. The capital's nightlife comes alive with friendly local pubs and bars creating a laid-back vibe. From enjoying live music to socializing with locals, Nuku'alofa nightlife delivers a fantastic balance of leisure and social interaction.

3. Shopping

Shopping in Nuku'alofa is an interesting experience, with markets and businesses selling a mix of traditional handicrafts and modern things. The Talamahu Market is a treasure mine of Tongan artifacts, handcrafted goods, and bright Tapa cloth. Visitors may browse local shops for stylish apparel, jewelry, and interesting gifts. The Handicraft Market is a must-visit for handmade traditional goods, offering an opportunity to support local artisans and take home a part of Tongan culture.

Vava'u Group

1. Islands and Beaches

The Vava'u Group, a magnificent archipelago in the north, has untouched islands and lonely beaches. The azure oceans around these islands are perfect for snorkeling and swimming. Popular places like Swallows Cave and Mariner's Cave give underwater thrills, exhibiting vibrant coral reefs and diverse aquatic life. Exploring remote islands, such as Mala Island, affords a calm reprieve with white sandy beaches and crystal-clear lagoons.

2. Water Activities

Vava'u is a paradise for water fanatics, presenting a diversity of activities. The tranquil and sheltered waters make it a perfect site for sailing and boat charters. Whale gazing is a prominent highlight, as Vava'u serves as a migratory path for humpback whales. Kayaking along the gorgeous canals and snorkeling in the vibrant coral gardens reveal the underwater magnificence that defines this collection of islands.

Ha'apai Group

1. Ecotourism and Nature Reserves

Ha'apai, the center island group, captivates nature aficionados with its pristine beauty and ecotourism possibilities. Landscapes filled with coconut palms and gorgeous beaches give a tranquil environment. The conservation efforts of Ha'apai are visible in sites like the Pangai Lagoon, a protected area that emphasizes the region's devotion to maintaining its natural beauty. Birdwatchers will find enjoyment in viewing the numerous bird species that occupy the islands.

2. Cultural Experiences

Ha'apai provides unique cultural experiences, allowing travelers to join with native cultures. Community-based tourism programs provide a chance to stay with local families, participate in traditional celebrations, and learn about Tongan culture. Visitors may watch traditional dances, attend village feasts, and obtain insights into the ordinary lives of the friendly Ha'apai communities.

'Eua Island

1. Hiking and Adventure

'Eua, famous for its rugged terrain and spectacular landscapes, is a haven for hiking fanatics. The 'Eua National Park has a network of pathways that lead to stunning vistas, historic caves, and cold waterfalls. The challenging 'Eua Coastal Cliffs trek gives beautiful perspectives of the Pacific Ocean. Exploring the island on foot immerses travelers in the natural beauty and varied ecosystems that define 'Eua.

2. Wildlife and Nature

'Eua is a refuge for nature, home to unusual plants and animals. Birdwatchers may uncover local species, like the unusual koki (Eua Lorikeet), while humpback whales frequent the oceans during various points of the year. 'Eua's diverse landscapes, from dense woodlands to limestone caves, make it a nature lover's dream, delivering a tranquil escape away from the hurry and bustle of modern life.

In summation, the areas inside Tonga illustrate the Kingdom's varied attractions, from the bustling capital of Nuku'alofa with its cultural remnants and vibrant marketplaces to the natural beauty of the Vava'u and Ha'apai groups, and the daring landscapes of 'Eua Island. Each area provides a particular experience, whether it is cultural immersion, water-based activities, or exploring the unspoiled beauty of Tonga's natural surroundings.

ACTIVITIES AND ADVENTURES

Snorkeling and Diving

Tonga's gorgeous oceans create an underwater paradise for snorkeling and diving fanatics. The archipelago is known for its stunning coral reefs, bursting with a rainbow of aquatic life. The coral gardens around the islands of Vava'u and Ha'apai create unusual landscapes, with colorful fish, rays, and even the uncommon reef shark.

Popular dive spots, such as the Cathedral in Vava'u, contain underwater caves and tunnels that give an intriguing dimension to the diving experience. For those unaccustomed to these activities, numerous operators in Tonga provide guided snorkeling and diving expeditions, allowing a safe and exciting exploration of the Kingdom's undersea wonders.

Whale Watching

Tonga ranks as one of the finest destinations for whale watching, specifically for the stunning humpback whales. These gentle giants migrate to Tonga's warm waters between July and October, affording it a rare opportunity to see their magnificent antics. Vava'u, in particular, is renowned for its role as a calving and breeding location for humpback whales.

Boat cruises and charters allow a chance to get up close and personal with these extraordinary creatures, giving a once-in-a-lifetime experience as they breach and play in the Pacific Ocean. The ethereal connection with nature during whale watching season is a highlight for many travelers visiting Tonga.

Cultural Festivals

Tonga's cultural vibrancy is best expressed via its vivid and authentic festivals. The Heilala Festival in June, honoring the birthday of the Tongan monarch, is a display of traditional dance, music, and majestic floats moving through Nuku'alofa.

The Pule'anga Fakatu'i'o, or Constitution Celebration, yearly in November, recognizes Tonga's independence and is a joyful expression of national pride. These events provide a thorough immersion into Tongan culture, allowing travelers to experience traditional costumes, complex dances, and the exuberant hospitality of the locals. Participating in these events creates a great reverence for the Kingdom's rich heritage.

Water Sports

For those wanting an adrenaline rush, Tonga offers an assortment of water activities that leverage its beautiful maritime environment. Kayaking over the tranquil seas of Vava'u offers visitors to traverse secluded coves and coral-filled lagoons.

Kitesurfing aficionados may harness the trade winds that sweep over the islands, notably at Ha'apai, delivering an exciting ride over the blue seas. Stand-up paddleboarding, windsurfing, and jet skiing are among popular sports in Tonga, guaranteeing that thrill-seekers may find their ideal water experience against the background of the Kingdom's stunning environment.

Trekking & Hiking

Tonga's various landscapes entice hikers and trekkers to experience its lush terrains and panoramic panoramas. 'Eua Island, in particular, is a trekking paradise with a network of routes that meander through lush woods, leading to clifftop vistas.

The 'Eua National Park gives opportunities for both beginner and expert hikers, with paths that include limestone caverns, ancient woods, and flowing waterfalls. In Ha'apai, the Tofua Caldera climb provides an adventurous trip to the rim of an active volcano, giving daring hikers awe-inspiring vistas of the volcanic scenery and surrounding oceans. These hiking trips not only exhibit Tonga's natural beauty but also give a meaningful connection with the environment and its different ecosystems.

In conclusion, Tonga's activities and adventures appeal to a broad variety of interests, ensuring that tourists may adapt their experiences to meet their tastes. Whether it's exploring the underwater wonders through snorkeling and diving, connecting with nature during whale watching season, immersing in cultural celebrations, engaging in thrilling water sports, or embarking on invigorating hikes, Tonga invites adventurers to discover the kingdom's unique blend of excitement and tranquility.

LOCAL CUISINE

Traditional Tongan Dishes

Tonga's culinary environment is a delightful blend of traditional Polynesian flavors, reflecting the kingdom's rich cultural heritage and dependency on locally derived resources. Traditional Tongan dishes are a celebration of the wealth of the land and sea, produced utilizing time-honored techniques that have been passed down through generations.

1. **Lu Sipi:** This famed Tongan meal comprises lamb or mutton, marinated and slow-cooked in an earth oven known as a 'umu. The meat is saturated with flavors from coconut cream, onions, and various aromatic herbs and spices.

2. Ota 'Ika: A tasty and tangy Tongan ceviche, Ota 'Ika consists of raw fish marinated in coconut cream, lime juice, onions, and other seasonings. The conclusion is a wonderful and spicy supper that highlights the abundance of fresh fish in Tongan waters.

3. 'Ufi: A starchy root vegetable, 'Ufi is often baked or boiled and consumed as a side dish. Its mild, nutty flavor accompanies meat and fish dishes, making it a fixture in Tongan cuisine.

4. Faikakai Topai: This coconut dumpling dessert is a wonderful delicacy adored by locals and visitors alike. Soft and doughy, these dumplings are often served with a drizzle of coconut cream and a dusting of sugar.

Popular Restaurants and Cafes

Tonga's culinary business has developed to encompass a variety of dining venues that cater to various palates, mixing traditional flavors with modern influences.

1. **Friends Café:** Located in Nuku'alofa, Friends Café is a popular restaurant that mixes a welcoming setting with a menu comprising a mix of Tongan and international dishes. The café's focus on employing fresh, local cuisine boosts the authenticity of its goods.

2. **Waterfront Café & Bar:** Situated along the waterfront in Vava'u, this establishment not only provides amazing views of the port but also serves a menu incorporating Tongan seafood delicacies. From grilled octopus to coconut-infused

fish dishes, Waterfront Café & Bar evokes the flavor of Tonga's coastal cuisine.

3. Bounty Bar & Restaurant: Nestled in Ha'apai, the Bounty Bar & Restaurant is famed for its laid-back environment and menu incorporating Tongan specialties. The establishment routinely hosts cultural events, giving a thorough dining experience immersed in local traditions.

Street Food and Local Markets

For a real feel of Tonga's culinary authenticity, witnessing the vibrant street food scene and local markets is a must.

1. Talamahu Market (Nuku'alofa): This vibrant market is a sensory feast, with sellers offering a range of fresh vegetables, seafood, and artisan handicrafts. Visitors may experience traditional Tongan delights like keke 'isite (coconut bread) or pick a quick and flavorful meal from one of the street food sellers.

2. Neiafu Market (Vava'u): Neiafu Market is a treasure trove of local delights, where travelers may enjoy freshly caught fish, tropical fruits, and traditional Tongan dishes. The market's lively environment offers a genuine look into daily life in Vava'u.

3. Pangai Market (Ha'apai): This local market in Ha'apai has a great assortment of fresh items, including tropical fruits and vegetables. Travelers may enjoy street gastronomic pleasures such as grilled fish skewers or taro chips, exhibiting the simplicity and deliciousness of Tonga's street gastronomy.

In conclusion, Tonga's culinary landscape is a reflection of the kingdom's cultural diversity and natural abundance. From the traditional flavors of lu sipi and ota 'ika to the innovative dishes in popular restaurants and the vibrant street food experiences in local markets, Tonga invites visitors to embark on a culinary journey that tantalizes the taste buds and fosters an appreciation for the richness of Tongan cuisine.

CULTURAL EXPERIENCES

Traditional Dance and Music

Tonga's cultural pulse is best conveyed via its traditional dance and music, a fascinating exhibition that depicts the rich history and customs of the country. The most significant traditional dance in Tonga is the Ma'ulu'ulu, defined by rhythmic dances, vibrant costumes, and the beautiful beat of drums and percussion instruments. Accompanied by harmonizing singing, these dances often reflect narratives of Tonga's history, including mythology, folklore, and daily life. Visitors get the option to observe these mesmerizing performances at cultural events, festivals, and even neighborhood gatherings, offering a full immersion into the creative expressions that comprise an important part of Tongan culture.

Arts and Crafts

Tonga's arts and crafts reflect the artistry and originality of its people, providing visitors an opportunity to take home true parts of Tongan culture. Tapa cloth, produced from the inner bark of the mulberry tree, is a traditional handicraft adorned with gorgeous designs and motifs. Local artisans beautifully produce woven objects, such as mats and baskets, employing traditional techniques passed down through generations.

The vibrant colors and distinctive forms of Tongan crafts generally match the natural beauty of the islands, making them not merely presents but tangible markers of Tonga's cultural past. Visitors may explore local markets and craft centers, engaging with craftspeople to acquire insights into the difficult process behind these handmade treasures.

Historical Sites and Museums

Tonga's historical sites and museums present a fascinating trip through the kingdom's past, providing a greater awareness of its cultural progress. The Tongan National Centre in Nuku'alofa is a cultural hub that features relics, photos, and exhibits reflecting the kingdom's history, notably its pre-European contact era. The Ha'amonga 'a Maui Trilithon, commonly referred to as the Stonehenge of the Pacific, stands as a mysterious archeological monument and a tribute to Tonga's old technological excellence.

Visiting the Langi tombs, and royal burial grounds, is a melancholy experience, affording insight into Tonga's royal past and the value of these hallowed resting places. Exploring these historical sites and museums allows travelers to follow Tonga's cultural narrative over the decades.

Meeting the Locals

One of the most pleasant features of visiting Tonga is the possibility of connecting with the warm and hospitable locals. Tongans are famous for their friendliness and friendly temperament, making it effortless for travelers to participate in actual interactions. Participating in a kava ceremony, a traditional social gathering where the ceremonial drink kava is shared, affords a unique chance to mingle with people and experience their convivial hospitality.

Attending community events, church services, or even indulging in a local feast known as a 'umu increases the cultural connection and enables visitors to form lasting memories of their time in Tonga. Meeting the people offers a wonderful glimpse into Tongan life, generating a sense of community and leaving travelers with cherished moments of shared laughter, storytelling, and traditions.

In conclusion, cultural interactions in Tonga are a multi-sensory excursion, including the rhythmic rhythms of traditional dancing, the meticulous craftsmanship of arts and crafts, the historical narratives contained in sites and museums, and the warm embrace of native hospitality. Whether witnessing a vibrant dance performance, selecting handmade souvenirs, exploring ancient archaeological sites, or forging connections with the locals, visitors to Tonga are invited to immerse themselves in a cultural tapestry that weaves together tradition, history, and the genuine warmth of the Kingdom's people.

PRACTICAL
INFORMATION

Emergency Contacts

Ensuring awareness of emergency contacts is vital for any tourist visiting a new location. In Tonga, the emergency services may be reached by phoning 911, and this number connects you to police, medical, and fire help. The police force of Tonga is normally polite and approachable, with the main police station being in Nuku'alofa, the capital city. Additionally, the local hospital and medical facilities are competent to address emergencies.

Healthcare Services: Vaiola Hospital in Nuku'alofa is the largest healthcare facility in Tonga, delivering medical services to residents and visitors alike. It's advisable to purchase travel insurance that covers medical emergencies to secure access to fast and comprehensive care.

Embassies and Consulates: Familiarize yourself with the location and contact information of your country's embassy or consulate in Tonga. In case of unplanned crises, having this information easily available could hasten help and support.

Local Transportation

Understanding the local transportation alternatives is crucial for touring the islands of Tonga successfully.

Inter-Island Flights: Domestic flights fly between the main island groups of Tongatapu, Vava'u, Ha'apai, and 'Eua. Real Tonga Airlines is the primary domestic airline, operating frequent flights that facilitate simple island-hopping.

Ferry Services: Ferries connect the main island of Tongatapu with Ha'apai and Vava'u. The ferry timing may vary, so it's crucial to check in advance and plan adequately.

Taxis and Rental Cars: Taxis are available in urban areas, and while they may not work on a metered system, it's essential to discuss pricing before beginning your journey. Rental vehicle services are also available, allowing flexibility for seeing the islands at your own pace.

Public Transportation: While public transportation is sparse, there are buses and small vans that travel on regular routes. These are cost-effective methods for moving modest distances within communities.

Internet and Communication

Staying connected during your travels in Tonga is simplified with several communication solutions.

Mobile Networks: Tonga offers mobile network coverage, and buying a local SIM card allows passengers to access internet plans and make calls. The main telecom providers are Digicel and TCC.

Internet Cafés: Internet cafés are available in urban areas, allowing a venue to use computers and access the Internet. However, connection speeds may vary, and it's essential to have a backup plan for critical online activities.

Wi-Fi Availability: Many hotels, resorts, and cafés give Wi-Fi connectivity, allowing travelers to stay connected. Keep in mind that in more remote places, internet access may be limited.

Banking and ATMs

Understanding the local banking system and the availability of ATMs permits uncomplicated financial transactions during your stay in Tonga.

Currency: The official currency of Tonga is the Tongan Pa'anga (TOP). Familiarize yourself with the current exchange rates, and it's advisable to carry a mix of cash and cards.

ATMs: ATMs are prevalent in large towns, particularly in Nuku'alofa. However, in certain remote districts, access to ATMs may be limited, hence it's suggested to withdraw cash in advance before heading to such locations.

Credit Cards: While major credit cards are accepted in urban areas and at select hotels and restaurants, cash is often employed across Tonga, especially in rural markets and smaller institutions.

Banking Hours: Banking hours in Tonga are typically from Monday to Friday, however select banks may operate on Saturday mornings. It's encouraged to conduct crucial financial activities during these hours.

In conclusion, being well-informed on practical facts such as emergency contacts, local transportation, internet and communication, and banking services improves the complete vacation experience in Tonga. By being prepared and educated, travelers may explore the islands with ease, providing a safe and joyful cruise through the heart of the South Pacific.

SUSTAINABLE TRAVEL

Responsible Tourism Practices

As visitors increasingly recognize the importance of sustainable and ethical tourism, Tonga stands out as a destination committed to safeguarding its natural and cultural heritage. Embracing ethical tourism practices is crucial for decreasing the impact of travel on the environment and local inhabitants.

1. Cultural Respect: Responsible tourists in Tonga foster cultural sensitivity. This entails knowing and obeying local norms, customs, and manners. Visitors are urged to acquire permission before taking images of individuals, especially in more secluded or traditional settlements.

2. Environmental Stewardship: The natural ecosystems of Tonga are a treasure to be conserved. Responsible tourists adhere to Leave No Trace guidelines, ensuring that natural locations remain undisturbed. This comprises proper waste disposal, lowering carbon footprints, and supporting conservation activities.

3. Support Local Economies: Contributing to local economies is an important part of ethical tourism. Visitors are invited to support local businesses, markets, and artists, ensuring that their travel expenditures have a good impact on the regions they visit. Purchasing locally-made souvenirs and engaging in community-based tourism programs helps sustain traditional livelihoods.

4. Wildlife Conservation: Tonga is home to diverse and varied marine and terrestrial animals. Responsible vacationers select activities that do not injure or annoy local animals. This encompasses ethical whale-watching practices, respecting nesting and breeding areas, and refraining from feeding or touching whales.

Conservation Efforts

Tonga's devotion to conservation is apparent in various programs aimed at safeguarding its natural resources and biodiversity. These measures are crucial for ensuring that future generations may continue to enjoy the kingdom's stunning landscapes and unique ecosystems.

1. Whale Sanctuary: Tonga has formed the Vava'u Environmental Protection Association, a non-profit organization concentrating on marine conservation, particularly in the Vava'u archipelago. This encompasses attempts to maintain the calving and breeding grounds of humpback whales, assuring their continuing presence in Tonga's waters.

2. Coral Reef conservation: The kingdom is actively interested in coral reef conservation, recognizing the value of these ecosystems for marine life and tourism. Initiatives include marine protected zones, coral planting operations, and public awareness campaigns to limit human effects on coral reefs.

3. Forest Conservation: The 'Eua National Park is a monument to Tonga's devotion to conserving its terrestrial biodiversity. Conservation projects focus on conserving local flora and fauna, notably unusual bird species. Sustainable hiking practices and ethical tourism concepts assist in the continuing success of these initiatives.

4. **Trash Management:** Tonga experiences challenges associated with waste management, particularly on smaller islands. Conservation organizations and local communities work together to promote waste reduction and recycling efforts. Responsible travelers play a role by minimizing single-use plastics and contributing to community clean-up projects.

Eco-Friendly Accommodations

Tonga presents a range of eco-friendly hotels that conform to the concepts of sustainable tourism. These institutions support environmental conservation, community engagement, and ethical tourism behaviors.

1. **Eco-Resorts:** Several eco-resorts in Tonga have adopted sustainable technologies, such as rainwater gathering, solar power, and trash reduction initiatives. These resorts typically integrate perfectly with their natural surroundings, presenting tourists with an immersive and environmentally responsible experience.

2. **Community Homestays:** Embracing the idea of community-based tourism, several accommodations in Tonga offer homestay experiences. Visitors receive the chance to stay with local families, join in daily activities, and receive insights into Tongan culture. The economic benefits of these homestays directly aid host communities.

3. Certification systems: Some motels in Tonga participate in recognized eco-certification initiatives. These programs assess and verify sustainable practices, guaranteeing that accommodations fit specified environmental and social standards. Certification lends trust to travelers seeking eco-friendly alternatives.

4. Conservation-Focused Lodges: Tonga is home to lodges and guesthouses that actively contribute to local conservation programs. These accommodations may provide educational programs, nature walks, or marine conservation activities for visitors, encouraging a better link between tourists and the natural environment.

In essence, sustainable tourism in Tonga comprises a collective effort to maintain the kingdom's cultural culture and natural beauty. Responsible tourist habits, conservation efforts, and eco-friendly hotels play key roles in maintaining Tonga's environment and ensuring that tourism maintains a constructive effect on local inhabitants. Visitors who accept these ideas aid the long-term survival of Tonga as a beloved destination in the South Pacific.

ESSENTIAL PHRASES AND LANGUAGE GUIDE

Basic Tongan Phrases

While English is generally recognized and spoken in Tonga, making an effort to acquire and employ simple Tongan words improves the cultural experience and fosters good interactions with locals. Here are key words to aid travelers in navigating conversations in the Kingdom of Tonga:

1. Greetings:

- Hello - Mālō e lelei
- Goodbye - Nofo ā
- How are you? - Fefe hake?
- I'm okay - 'Oku sai

2. Politeness:

- Please - Fakamolemole
- Thank you - Mālō
- You're welcome - 'Oku ou sai

3. Asking for Help:

- Excuse me - Tolongo
- Help! - Fake Mo'oni!
- I don't understand - 'Oku ikai ha'u 'i he lea

4. Directions:

- Where is...? - 'I fe mo...?
- Left - Mali'e Right - 'Ua

5. Numbers:

- One - Taha
- Two - Fua
- Three - Tolu
- Four - Fā
- Five - Nima

6. Common Expressions:

- Yes - 'Io
- No - 'Ikai
- I'm sorry - Tulou
- Good - Lelei
- Bad - Tokoni

7. Food and Drink:

- Water - Vaai
- Food - Me'a'ai
- Delicious - Anga'ofē

8. Time:

- Today - 'I he 'aho ni
- Yesterday - 'Ua na'a
- Tomorrow - 'Apongipongi

Useful Translations

Understanding important translations is helpful for tourists managing everyday activities, communicating with people, and appreciating the cultural subtleties of Tonga.

1. Transportation:

- Airport - Lupepau'u
- Boat - Vaka
- Bus - Pāsí
- Car - Kā

2. Accommodation:

- Hotel - Hōtelí
- Guesthouse - Fale fakataha
- Room - Lomu

3. Emergencies:

- Emergency - 'Urgensí
- Doctor - To'asā
- Police - Pule'anga

4. Shopping:

- Market - Mākeisi
- Money - Pa'anga
- How much does it cost? - Fēfē hake 'i
  he tokotaha koē 'eni?

5. Health:

- Pharmacy - Pēkesí
- Hospital - Hōpītale
- Medicine - Lāví

6. Leisure:

- Beach - 'Aho
- Tour - Tā
- Swimming - Sivimi

7. Nature:

- Mountain - Ma'ama'a
- Ocean - Moana
- Tree - Ngaahi

8. Miscellaneous:

- Post Office - 'Ofeesi faka'amelie
- Telephone - Telefoni
- Internet - 'Initaneti

Learning and applying these fundamental words and translations not only helps conversation but also reflects a genuine interest in Tongan culture. Locals appreciate the effort, and it typically leads to more stimulating and meaningful encounters throughout your time in the Kingdom of Tong

Recommended Reading

Exploring Tonga's rich cultural, historical, and environmental legacy may be improved with intelligent reading. Here are some suggested works that give excellent insights into the Kingdom of Tonga:

1. "Tonga: A New Bibliography" by Ian C. Campbell:

This thorough bibliography provides a plethora of information for anyone interested in diving further into Tonga's history, culture, and social dynamics. It provides an ideal beginning place for academic inquiry and cultural knowledge.

2. "Tonga - A Travel Survival Kit" by Paul Smitz:

Written by a seasoned travel writer, this handbook gives practical advice for tourists, including information on lodging, transit, and cultural etiquette. It acts as a convenient companion for people planning a journey to Tonga.

3. "The Friendly Islands: 1616 to 1900" by E. Wood-Ellem:

This historical text dives into Tonga's history, encompassing the time from the early interactions with European explorers until the start of the 20th century. It gives a thorough overview of the Kingdom's dealings with the outside world.

4. "The Whale Rider" by Witi Ihimaera:

While not explicitly centered on Tonga, this book by Witi Ihimaera delivers a captivating tale set in the larger Polynesian environment. It addresses issues of tradition, identity, and the link between people and the environment.

Useful Websites and Apps

Navigating the digital world may substantially improve the trip experience. Here are some helpful websites and applications for anyone considering a vacation to Tonga:

1. Tonga Tourism Website:
The official tourist website offers detailed information on lodgings, activities, and travel suggestions. It's a fantastic resource for organizing your schedule and getting current on travel-related concerns.

2. Real Tonga Airlines:

For domestic flights between the several island groups, Real Tonga Airlines' website offers a trusted platform for monitoring flight schedules, purchasing tickets, and making travel plans.

3. Maps.me:

This offline mapping program is especially handy when visiting Tonga, where internet availability may be restricted in certain locations. Download the maps for Tonga in advance to travel with ease.

4. Tonga Broadcasting Commission:

Stay updated about local news and events with the Tonga Broadcasting Commission's website. It gives information on current affairs, cultural events, and more.

In conclusion, using suggested reading, helpful websites, apps, maps, and guides may considerably improve the entire travel experience in Tonga. These tools not only give essential information but also act as companions for tourists looking to dig into the varied facets of Tongan culture, history, and natural beauty.

CONCLUSION

Recap and Highlights

As we complete our thorough guide to Tonga, let's take time to summarize the features that make the Kingdom of Tonga a unique and intriguing destination for visitors seeking a combination of natural beauty, rich culture, and kind hospitality.

1. **Unique Cultural Experiences:** Tonga's cultural tapestry is woven with traditional dances, colorful music, and local rituals that urge tourists to immerse themselves in a rich and genuine Polynesian history. Engaging in traditional rites, partaking in festivals, and meeting people are unforgettable ways to interact with Tonga's cultural richness.

2. Pristine Natural Beauty: The Kingdom of Tonga presents an untamed paradise with blue oceans, beautiful landscapes, and various ecosystems. From the gorgeous beaches of Vava'u to the volcanic landscapes of 'Eua, every island provides a distinct combination of natural treasures. Exploring coral reefs, witnessing humpback whales, and walking through jungles give unrivaled experiences for nature aficionados.

3. Adventure and Activities: Tonga offers a range of explorers with activities such as snorkeling, diving, whale watching, and trekking. The crystal-clear seas encourage exploration, and the different landscapes form a playground for people seeking both adrenaline-pumping experiences and calm getaways.

4. Sustainable Travel Commitment: Tonga's focus on sustainability is obvious in its conservation activities, eco-friendly lodgings, and responsible tourism practices. Visitors have the chance to contribute positively to the preservation of the Kingdom's natural and cultural assets.

5. Tongan Cuisine and Hospitality: The tastes of Tongan cuisine, combined with local products and culinary traditions, present a delicious trip for food connoisseurs. Traditional delicacies like lu sipi and ota 'ika display native tastes, while the friendly welcome of the Tongan people provides a welcoming ambiance for tourists.

Inviting Visitors to Explore Tonga

Tonga offers a warm welcome to tourists seeking a location that goes beyond the ordinary, providing a voyage of exploration, connection, and restoration.

1. Embrace the Local Spirit: Venture beyond the well-trodden roads and immerse yourself in the real essence of Tonga. Attend local festivals, partake in traditional traditions, and appreciate the real kindness of the Tongan people. The Kingdom's cultural diversity is best experienced via meaningful encounters.

2. Discover Hidden Gems: Explore the different sceneries and hidden jewels dotted around the islands. Whether it's the isolated beaches of Ha'apai, the underwater marvels of Vava'u, or the mountainous trails of 'Eua, each place displays a new side of Tonga's natural splendor. Take the time to explore these hidden gems.

3. Contribute to Sustainability: As you visit the Kingdom, be conscious of your ecological imprint. Support eco-friendly lodgings, engage in conservation activities, and embrace responsible tourist practices. Contributing to sustainability means that future generations may continue to experience Tonga's natural landscapes.

4. Indulge in Culinary Delights: Let your taste buds appreciate the tastes of Tonga. From traditional feasts to tasting street cuisine at local markets, the gastronomic adventure in Tonga is a celebration of local ingredients and cultural variety. Engage in the culinary experiences that highlight the Kingdom's gastronomic treasures.

5. Create Lasting Memories: Tonga is a canvas for crafting unforgettable memories. Whether it's viewing the gorgeous humpback whales, visiting old archeological sites, or just soaking in the calm of the islands, each experience becomes a part of a unique and beloved travel tale.

In conclusion, Tonga urges tourists to go on an adventure that exceeds the ordinary. With its dedication to conserving its cultural and ecological legacy, Tonga welcomes tourists to not simply see but actively engage in the kingdom's narrative. As you visit this Pacific paradise, may your trips to Tonga be full of discovery, connection, and the creation of memories that last a lifetime. Mālō 'aupito! (Thank you very much!)

Printed in Great Britain
by Amazon